Hang Gliding

by K. C. Kelley

Published by The Child's World®
1980 Lookout Drive
Mankato, MN 56003-1705
800-599-READ
www.childsworld.com

The Child's World®: Mary Berendes, Publishing Director
Shoreline Publishing Group, LLC: James Buckley Jr.,
   Production Director
The Design Lab: Design and production

ISBN: 978-1-60973-208-0
LCCN: 2011928882

Photo credits: Cover: iStock.
Interior: AP/Wide World: 23; Corbis: 8, 9, 20, 27, 28;
dreamstime.com: Ernst Daniel Scheffler 12, Richard
Sheppard 16; Photos.com: 7, 11, 15, 19.

Printed in the United States of America
Mankato, Minnesota
July, 2011
PA02094

Table of Contents

This statue of Icarus shows the wings that let him down.

CHAPTER ONE

Up, Up in the Air!

A story told by **ancient** Greeks shows how much humans want to fly. An inventor named Daedalus built large wings made of wax and feathers. He was able to fly from cliffs and glide through the air. His son, Icarus, made his own set of wings. The son wanted to fly even higher than his father. Daedalus warned Icarus that the sun would melt the wax if he flew too high. Icarus ignored his dad. He flew too high, the wax melted . . . and Icarus fell into the sea.

But that's just a story. In real life, people did figure out how to fly like birds. People tried lots of ways to "grow" wings like birds. The Italian inventor Leonardo da Vinci was one of many who drew pictures of wings and gliders. Finally, in the late 1800s, Otto Lilienthal of Germany designed a large winged glider. He guided it through the air—but not very high—on hundreds of flights. His work led to the creation of airplanes with powerful engines.

Otto Lilienthal's gliders set the stage for the Wright brothers.

Rogallo shows off a model of his wing (right).
The drawing below shows how he thought gliders
could be used to help space capsules land.

Birds, of course, don't need engines. Even as airplanes took to the sky, the idea of flying without power from an engine stuck around. In 1948, American scientist Francis Rogallo designed a new kind of wing. **NASA**, the U.S. space agency, looked at the wings when they were building spaceships in the 1960s. The wing didn't end up on spaceships, but fans of flying saw another use.

In 1971, strapped beneath a Rogallo wing, Tom Dickinson flew his glider about 300 feet. Daedalus would have been impressed.

From then, better and better gliders have been created. The sport of hang gliding makes the dream of flying real. Thousands of people swoop off cliffs or hills and ride the wind. They come as close as possible to seeing things as birds do.

Today's hang gliders are usually based on the Rogallo wing. They are made of aluminum and covered with fabric. The flyer hangs below in a bag. That's why it's called hang gliding!

A **similar** sport called paragliding uses a type of parachute. Instead of lying down, the flyers are in a seat that hangs below the chute. Paragliders, like hang gliders, take off from their feet and float on wind and air currents.

Whether beneath a wing or a parachute, flyers are proving that the sky is not just for the birds.

A view from below shows how the pilot hangs beneath the glider wing.

CHAPTER TWO

Hang Gliding Basics

The most important gear for a hang glider pilot is, of course, a hang glider. The length of a glider's wings depends on the pilot's size and weight. Bigger pilots would use bigger wings. However, more experienced pilots can use smaller wings sometimes. Most gliders are from 16 to 24 feet (4.9 to 7.3 m) wide. The shape of the wing is formed by a frame of aluminum tubes. Nylon is stretched over the frame. The nylon can come in almost any color, just as birds' feathers can.

At takeoff, the pilot balances the wide wings to keep it level.

Hanging from the center of the wing is a **harness** or bag. The pilot is strapped into the harness face down, with his or her feet pointing backward. The most common type of hang glider also has a triangle of tubes hanging point-up from the center of the wing. The pilot uses the bottom of this triangle to help control the glider in flight.

Hang glider pilots wear helmets to protect them during takeoff and landing. Many wear goggles due to wind in their face. Some also wear **altimeters**, which tell how high a person is above the ground.

Look for the metal triangle that the pilot uses to steer.

Perhaps the hardest thing to learn in hang gliding is how to take off. It looks as simple as running down a hill until the wind catches the wing. But it takes a bit of bravery to launch into the air from a hill. That's why training with an expert is very important for beginning pilots.

Once in the air, a hang glider pilot uses his or her body to do most of the steering. By leaning left or right, he can turn the glider. Pushing down or up on the metal bar (the bottom of the triangle) causes the glider to sink or rise.

After takeoff, this pilot will put his feet into the blue pack to help his balance.

Without an engine to power them, how do hang gliders stay in the air? The answer lies in the air itself. Glider pilots look for two kinds of "lift," or air currents that are going upward. The air, going up, carries the wing and the rider upward.

The two basic types of lift are called ridge and **thermal**. Ridge lift happens when wind hits a hill or cliff. The wind, bouncing upward from the hill, creates an area of lift. You often see hang gliders floating above cliffs or hillsides.

Thermal lift happens because warmer air rises. When glider pilots—or birds—find a pocket of this warmer air, they can float on it for hours. Thermal lifts usually come in tall columns of air moving up from the ground. A glider pilot can soar around and around in this column, just as a bird of prey might float on a thermal over a meadow.

This paraglider uses ridge lift to float easily along.

Packing Up

Hang gliders can be taken apart after they are used. Pilots can usually pack the tubes into a bag. They fold up the wing fabric and harness. Putting together and taking apart a glider takes a bit of time. However, it means pilots can travel to many places to try their favorite sport.

Landing is also tricky, but can be mastered. A hang glider can land anywhere that is pretty flat. The pilot slowly guides the glider lower and lower. They try to come in at a low angle, rather than a steep one. As they get just above the ground, they push forward on the control bar. This "stalls," or stops the glider and pilots can put their feet down, running to a stop and lowering the glider to the ground.

Landing a hang glider: The key is pushing the nose up at the right time.

CHAPTER THREE

High Above It All

Most hang gliders do their sport for the joy of flying. They might also join clubs to meet other flyers. Some hang gliders take part in competitions. Events are held all over the U.S. as well as in other countries. A world championship is held every year as well. Pilots compete over a course, trying to complete turns in the shortest time.

In 2010, Austrian pilot Manfred Ruhmer continued to be the best in the world. He won his fifth World Championship, which was held in Germany. At that event, the winds were too strong on the day the women's events were to be held. The 2009 women's champion was Corinna Schwiegerhausen from Germany.

World champion Manfred Ruhmer
steers through a race course.

This pilot adds streamers and smoke to his glider for a cool display.

Ruhmer also has his name in the record book. In 2001, he flew a hang glider 435 miles (700.6 km) over Texas. An American flyer, Larry Tudor, set a long-standing hang glider record. His flight to 2.7 miles (4,343 m) is still the highest ever.

Hang gliders don't usually go very fast. The slow flight to let pilots look down at the world is one of the joys of the sport. However, speed records are kept. Dustin Martin of the U.S. reached 31 miles per hour (49.8 kph) in 2009.

Along with setting records, some hang gliders try **aerobatics** (air-ah-BA-tix). These loops and spins are like gymnastics in the air. Very talented pilots can even do a complete loop, though this is a very dangerous move.

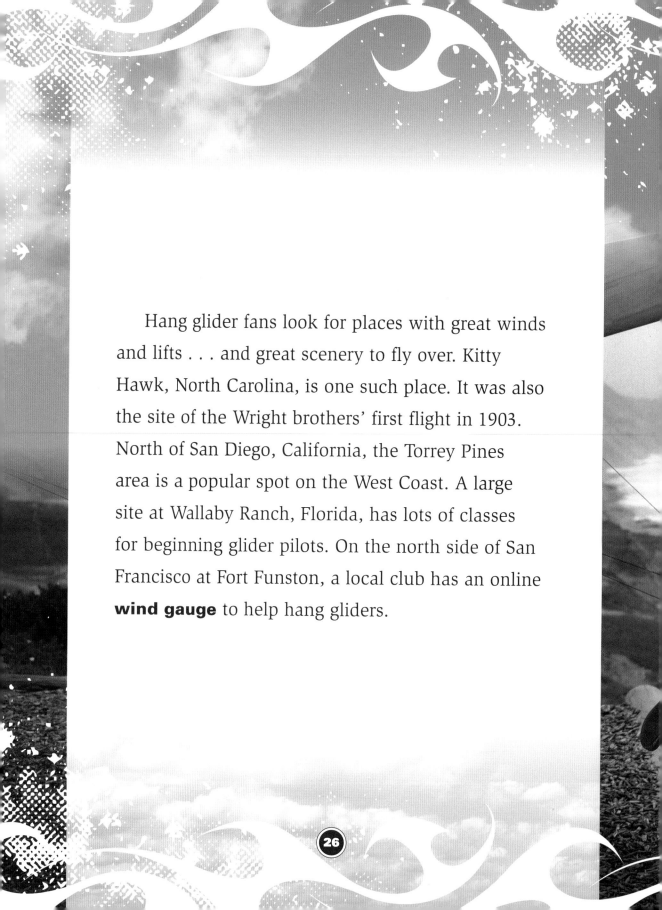

Hang glider fans look for places with great winds and lifts . . . and great scenery to fly over. Kitty Hawk, North Carolina, is one such place. It was also the site of the Wright brothers' first flight in 1903. North of San Diego, California, the Torrey Pines area is a popular spot on the West Coast. A large site at Wallaby Ranch, Florida, has lots of classes for beginning glider pilots. On the north side of San Francisco at Fort Funston, a local club has an online **wind gauge** to help hang gliders.

Flying Two by Two
Most hang gliders fly **solo**. However, when training, they can fly together with an instructor. Other flyers just enjoy having company in the sky. Special harnesses help two people fly together, usually side by side.

Gliders at Fort Funston soar out over the Pacific Ocean.

Hang gliding can give pilots amazing bird's-eye views.

Hang gliding can take pilots far above the world, flying with the birds. It can also take them to beautiful places around the world. Australia, with its wide open spaces, has many hang gliding fans. In Europe, several spots in France and Switzerland draw hang gliders in. In Guatemala, hang gliders can soar above a volcano (don't worry . . . it's not active!).

One thing hang gliders don't do is fly too close to the sun. They've all read about Icarus!

Glossary

aerobatics—gymnastic-like moves done in an aircraft

altimeters—devices that measure distance above the ground

ancient—very, very old

harness—a set of straps that hold a person in place

NASA—the National Aeronautics and Space Administration, the U.S. group that organizes space travel

similar—very much alike

solo—alone

thermal—having to do with heat

wind gauge—a device that measure the speed of the wind

Find Out More

BOOKS

Eyewitness Flight
By Andrew Nahum. New York, NY: DK Children, 2011.
A photo-packed book about all the ways that people fly, including hang gliders. Diagrams show how wings work and how such heavy things stay in the air!

Hang Gliding and Parasailing
By John Schindler. Milwaukee, WI: Gareth Stevens, 2005.
More details about these two high-flying sports.

WEB SITES

For links to learn more about extreme sports: **childsworld.com/links**

Note to Parents, Teachers, and Librarians: We routinely verify our Web links to make sure they are safe and active sites. So encourage your readers to check them out!

Index

About the Author

K. C. Kelley prefers to fly in things with motors, but he's also the author of sports books for young readers, he has written about baseball, football, basketball, and soccer, as well as books about animals, astronauts, and other cool stuff.